D1607002

MAKO SHARKS

by Julie Murray

Cody Koala
An Imprint of Pop!
popbooksonline.com

Hello! My name is
Cody Koala

This book is filled with videos, puzzles, games, and more! Scan the QR codes* while you read, or visit the website below to make this book pop.

popbooksonline.com/mako

*Scanning QR codes requires a web-enabled smart device with a QR code reader app and a camera.

abdobooks.com

Published by Pop!, a division of ABDO, PO Box 398166, Minneapolis, Minnesota 55439. Copyright ©2024 by Abdo Consulting Group, Inc. International copyrights reserved in all countries. No part of this book may be reproduced in any form without written permission from the publisher. Cody Koala™ is a trademark and logo of Pop!.

Printed in the United States of America, North Mankato, Minnesota.

052023
082023

THIS BOOK CONTAINS
RECYCLED MATERIALS

Cover Photo: Getty Images
Interior Photos: Shutterstock; Getty Images; Blue Planet Archive
Editors: Elizabeth Andrews and Grace Hansen
Series Designer: Victoria Bates

Library of Congress Control Number: 2022950511

Publisher's Cataloging-in-Publication Data
Names: Murray, Julie, author.
Title: Mako sharks / by Julie Murray
Description: Minneapolis, Minnesota : Pop!, 2024 | Series: Sharks | Includes online resources and index
Identifiers: ISBN 9781098244255 (lib. bdg.) | ISBN 9781098244958 (ebook)
Subjects: LCSH: Mako sharks--Juvenile literature. | Sharks--Juvenile literature. | Sharks--Behavior--Juvenile literature. | Marine fishes--Behavior--Juvenile literature.
Classification: Classification: DDC 598.47--dc23

Two Kinds

Mako sharks live in **tropical** and **temperate** oceans around the world. They swim near the water's surface far from shore. Mako sharks are **migratory** animals.

Table of Contents

Chapter 1
Two Kinds 4

Chapter 2
Built for Speed 8

Chapter 3
Ocean Hunters 14

Chapter 4
Life of a Mako Shark 18

Making Connections 22
Glossary 23
Index 24
Online Resources 24

Mako sharks can swim more than 35 miles (56km) in a day.

Watch a video here!

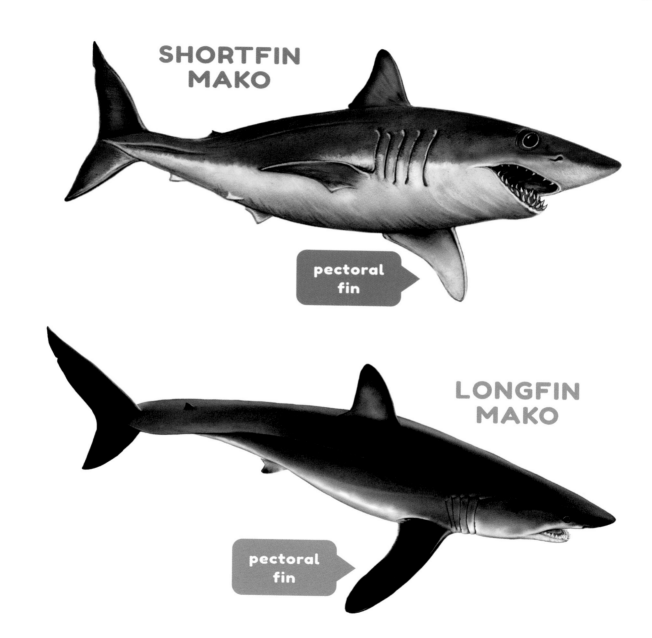

SHORTFIN MAKO

pectoral fin

LONGFIN MAKO

pectoral fin

There are two kinds of mako sharks. The main difference between shortfin mako sharks and longfin mako sharks is the size of their pectoral fins. Longfin makos also have slimmer bodies.

Mako sharks are one of the few sharks that can **regulate** their internal body temperature.

Chapter 2

Built for Speed

Mako sharks are built for speed! Their bodies are shaped like bullets. Shortfin makos are the fastest sharks in the ocean. They can swim 60 mph (96.6kph)!

Learn more here!

Mako sharks are
blue-gray in color.
Their bellies
are white.

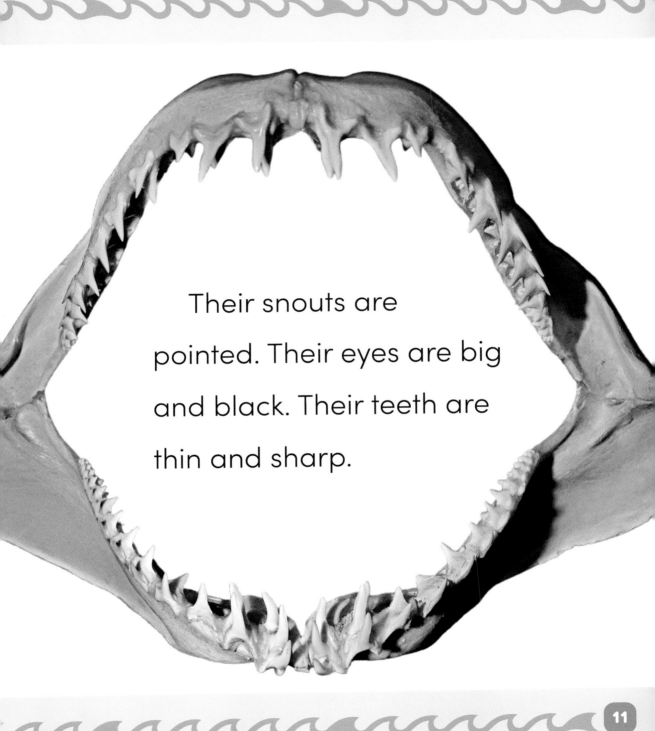

Their snouts are pointed. Their eyes are big and black. Their teeth are thin and sharp.

caudal
fin

The mako shark has a **crescent**-shaped caudal fin.

Mako sharks can grow eight to 14 feet (2.4 to 4.3m) long. They can weigh more than 1,000 pounds (453.6kg). Females are usually larger than males.

Chapter 3

Ocean Hunters

Mako sharks are fierce hunters. They **ambush** their **prey** from below. Mako sharks bite their prey. Then they swallow pieces whole.

Explore links here!

Mako sharks use their excellent senses of sight and smell to hunt. They like to eat swordfish and sailfish. They also eat turtles, dolphins, and squid.

Chapter 4

Life of a Mako Shark

Mako sharks give birth to young called pups. Between two and 30 pups can be born in a litter. Pups are on their own after they are born. They can live up to 30 years in the wild.

Complete an activity here!

Mako sharks are very smart and put up quite a fight when caught on a fishing line. Due to overfishing, mako shark populations have declined. Protecting mako sharks is important.

Making Connections

Text-to-Self

Imagine you are fishing on a boat in the ocean. Would you like to catch a mako shark? Why or why not?

Text-to-Text

Have you read a book about a different kind of shark? How is that shark like a mako shark? How is it different?

Text-to-World

Mako sharks are very smart. Can you think of another animal that is intelligent?

Glossary

ambush – a surprise attack from a hidden position.

crescent – the shape of the moon when it looks like a narrow arc.

migratory – pertaining to migration or the act of migrating. To migrate is to move from one place to another.

prey – an animal that is hunted by other animals for food.

regulate – to adjust or control.

temperate – relating to an area where average temperatures range between 50 and 55 degrees Fahrenheit (10 and 13°C).

tropical – relating to an area with an average temperature above 77 degrees Fahrenheit (25°C) where no freezing occurs.

Index

baby mako sharks, 18

body, 8, 10, 13

color, 10

eyes, 11

food, 17

habitat, 4

hunting, 14, 17

lifespan, 18

longfin mako, 6–7

shortfin mako, 6–8

size, 13

snout, 11

speed, 8

teeth, 11

Online Resources

popbooksonline.com

Thanks for reading this Cody Koala book!

This book is filled with videos, puzzles, games, and more! Scan the QR codes* while you read, or visit the website below to make this book pop.

popbooksonline.com/mako

*Scanning QR codes requires a web-enabled smart device with a QR code reader app and a camera.